101
DOG ILLUSTRATIONS

A Pictorial Archive of Championship Breeds

Gladys Emerson Cook

DOVER PUBLICATIONS, INC.
Mineola, New York

ACKNOWLEDGMENTS

I wish to give credit to the photographers Evelyn Shafer, William Brown, R. Tauskey, and Joan Ludwig for their excellent photographs of champion dogs on which some of the lithographs are based; to *Popular Dogs* for the use of their book, *Visualizations of the Dog Standards;* and to Ab Sidewater for his advice. I wish to express my gratitude to Arthur Frederick Jones of the *Kennel Gazette,* a friend with unexcelled knowledge of dogs, for his valuable aid and advice in compiling this book. Credit goes also to the American Kennel Club, *The Complete Dog Book,* Newly Revised Edition, 1961, the bible for dog breeders, on which the descriptive material on the breeds is based. *Animal Locomotion* (1887), by Edward Muybridge, was a great aid in the sketches of the dog running.

G. E. C.

Bibliographical Note

This Dover edition, first published in 2007, is an unabridged republication of *All Breeds, All Champions: A Book of Dogs,* by Gladys Emerson Cook, originally published by Harper & Row, New York, in 1962.

International Standard Book Number: 0-486-45438-X

Manufactured in the United States of America
Dover Publications, Inc., 31 East 2nd Street, Mineola, N.Y. 11501

AN APPRECIATION

It has been a distinct privilege to see in advance of publication the outstanding series of dog portraits done by Gladys Emerson Cook, for this is the finest collection among many good ones that she has finished in the course of a relatively few years.

Dog portraiture is one of the most challenging forms of art for it entails not only a keen eye to set down faithfully the points of a dog's breed but the subtleties that make the specimen an individual within that breed. Miss Cook's dogs all have their own personalities; their eyes and their expressions are their own—they seem ready to "speak" and move. Perhaps this is because, unlike so many of today's artists who appear to be lost without a camera to record details, she prefers to work from the living specimen. To her it is a disappointment when she is forced by distance to work the other way.

This book should enhance her position as one of America's foremost artists specializing in dogs. Her dogs have personality but they also have correct texture of coat, proper proportions, and breed type. It is a superb job from first page to last.

CLASSIFICATION OF BREEDS

To those who deem mysterious the division of America's purebred dogs into six variety groups, it is pointed out that there is nothing new about the classification of breeds. One of the earliest writers on the subject was Xenophon who, in 400 B.C., not only divided the then-known breeds into classes but wrote extensively and in detail on the work of the various dogs—especially those used for different forms of hunting. Thus we know that classification goes back at least twenty-three centuries. However, the most extensive early classification of dogs was in the days of Roman glory, just before the start of the Christian Era. Curiously, the Romans also divided their dogs into six groups, and four of those early divisions correspond to modern variety groups. The Romans had (1) house dogs, (2) shepherd dogs, (3) sporting dogs, (4) war dogs, (5) dogs that hunted by scent, and (6) dogs that hunted by sight.

The American Kennel Club, for the purpose of judging at its shows, has six divisions as follows: Group I, Sporting Dogs, comprising the breeds used in hunting with guns; Group II, Hounds, which takes in both the scent and the sight hunters; Group III, Working Dogs, including not only all the breeds used as shepherds' or drovers' helpers but also those designated as war dogs by the Romans; Group IV, Terriers, roughly most of the breeds used to follow into the burrows of foxes and other game animals that take refuge in the ground—i.e., a dog that will "go to ground"; Group V, Toys, in many cases miniatures of dogs found in other groups and kept only as pets; Group VI, Non-Sporting Dogs, kept principally as pets but including some breeds that were once widely known for their usefulness.

At shows held under American Kennel Club rules the dogs chosen by the judges as "best of breed," or as "best of variety" in certain cases, then enter competition for "best in group." The six dogs that take first place in the groups then compete for "best in show."

Arthur Frederick Jones
Editor of *The Kennel Gazette*

CONTENTS

SPORTING DOGS

Wirehaired Pointing Griffon

WIREHAIRED POINTING GRIFFON
Often regarded as a breed from France, the Wirehaired Pointing Griffon was actually bred in Holland in the 1870's by E. K. Korthals, the son of a wealthy banker. Later Korthals carried on his work with breeding in France and Germany, where he extolled his dog's virtues, especially the keen nose and the ability to point and retrieve game. This dog is adaptable to swamp country because of its harsh coat, and is a strong swimmer and water retriever. It is widely supposed to be of Setter, Spaniel and Otter Hound blood, and a cross with the German Shorthaired Pointer is evident. The Griffon's hair forms a mustache and eyebrows, and he has a lively and gay air. Height, 19½ to 23½ inches.

POINTER   The Pointer was the first dog used to point game. This breed originated in England and is a mixture of Foxhound, Greyhound, and Bloodhound, and doubtless the "Setting Spaniel," which was the progenitor of all bird dogs. The Pointer of today is distinctly a gun dog. He is muscular and lithe, clean-limbed, full of energy and joy of the hunt. His speed, endurance, courage, and concentration on his job make him an ideal dog for the field. At the age of two months he is already pointing. The usual color is white with liver markings but he can be orange and white or black and white. His coat must be very short and have a sheen. Even-tempered, sensible, and affectionate, the Pointer is a good companion both in the field and at home. Wide variations of size and weight are allowable provided balance and symmetry are right for muscularity and coordination.

Pointer

Pointer at work

GERMAN SHORTHAIRED POINTER

This breed is a combination of the old Spanish Pointer, the English Foxhound, and the Bloodhound. With his keen scent he has developed into a pointing bird dog, effective in night hunting; retrieving on land and in water is a strong part of his nature. He is equally valuable as a watchdog and friend. He works with all kinds of game from birds through rabbit and opossum to deer. His coat is water-resistant and his feet are webbed, making it easy for him to retrieve in rough country and icy water. Height 21 to 25 inches at shoulder; weight 45 to 75 pounds.

GERMAN WIREHAIRED POINTER

Intelligent and determined, this dog is definitely a Pointer and has a lively manner and a sturdy build. He is rather aloof but not unfriendly. Combined in his breed are the traits of the Foxhound, Pointer, and Poodle. The German Wirehair points and retrieves equally well on land and in the water. He has a very keen nose, a tough constitution, and a stiff, wiry coat, flat-lying but long enough to shield his body and protect him in all sorts of bad weather. Usually his color is liver and white, with brown nose and head. Height at withers 22 to 26 inches.

German Shorthaired Pointer

German Wirehaired Pointer

CHESAPEAKE BAY RETRIEVER   This dog is a true American, having originated around the Chesapeake Bay area. After considerable crossbreeding, a definite type was developed by about 1885. It showed great adaptability in the rough, icy waters of the Chesapeake and was able to retrieve hundreds of ducks a day. The dog's coat should be thick and short and the color of dead grass. Its texture is important as the oil in the harsh outer coat and woolly undercoat helps keep the cold water from reaching the dog's skin. This breed is courageous, alert, intelligent, has a love of water and a good disposition, and makes a fine companion and worker. The Flat-Coated and Curly-Coated Retrievers are the most important outcrosses of the breed. Height, 21 to 26 inches; weight, 55 to 75 pounds.

Chesapeake Bay Retriever

Chesapeake Bay Retriever and Duck

CURLY-COATED RETRIEVER   The Curly-Coated Retriever is supposed to be descended from the English Water Spaniel, the retrieving Setter, and the Irish Water Spaniel. Later the St. John's Newfoundland and the Poodle were added to the crossing, giving his coat a tight curl—the coat should be a mass of crisp curls all over in liver or black. He is considered easy to train, of great endurance, affectionate and hardy, and he loves the water. He makes delightful company and a good guard dog.

FLAT-COATED RETRIEVER   This dog was for the most part developed in England and he dates back to 1860. He is both a natural water dog, retrieving and delivering with a commendable style, and excellent for upland shooting. He is the only Retriever that points and is an all-round gun dog. The original cross was from the Labrador Retriever and the St. John's Newfoundland; the Gordon Setter and the Irish Setter have been added. The coat, usually wholly black, is close-lying, wavy, and dense, and gives protection in the water. Weight, 60 to 70 pounds.

GOLDEN RETRIEVER   These dogs came into prominence in England during the early part of the nineteenth century. They are the result of the crossing of the Gordon Setter, the St. John's Newfoundland, and later the Tweed Water Spaniel, which was light liver in color. The Golden is sensitive and gentle, quick to learn and a willing worker, both in water and with upland birds. He should have a thick waterproof undercoat to withstand cold temperature and icy water. His height is from 21½ to 24 inches, his weight from 60 to 75 pounds.

Curly-Coated Retriever

Flat-Coated Retriever

Golden Retriever

Golden Retriever and Duck

LABRADOR RETRIEVER   This Retriever actually came from New-foundland rather than Labrador. His coat should be close so that it sheds water easily. The tail should be similar to an otter's, short and thick at the stump, with the hair divided underneath. The eye color is light brown, similar to the color of burnt sugar. The coat is black, yellow, or chocolate. The dogs are great retrievers both on land and in the water, and in England a Labrador must have received a working certificate to be a champion. The general form is stocky and sturdy, with a very active look. Height at shoulder, 21½ to 24½ inches, weight 55 to 70 pounds.

Labrador Retriever

Labrador Retriever and Duck

Yellow Labrador Retriever

ENGLISH SETTER As long as four hundred years ago English Setters were trained bird dogs, and they have been popular favorites ever since. They were produced from crosses of the Spanish Pointer, the large Water Spaniel, and the Springer Spaniel. The appearance of dignity and elegance combined with a sweetness of disposition make them excellent home and field dogs, especially in the suburbs and country—for the English Setter needs plenty of action and exercise. The color varies widely, black, white, tan, or blue or orange belton or flecked mixtures. The tail should be straight and tapering, with the feathers straight and silky. Height, 24 to 25 inches, weight 50 to 70 pounds.

GORDON SETTER Gordon Setters go back at least to 1620 but came especially into favor in the kennels of the Duke of Gordon in Scotland in the late 1700's. They are black-and-tan in coloring, and have beauty, brains, and bird sense. With this breed there is no distinction between field and show types. Bench show champions are used regularly for hunting. The Gordon is a true Setter, resembling the English and Irish Setters in general type only. The coat is silky black with rich mahogany markings. The Gordon's beauty is outstanding in the field, his tail wagging gaily as he seeks out a bird. He is a very devoted and loyal dog to his human family. He usually loves children and acts as an excellent guard dog. Height at shoulders 23 to 27 inches, weight 45 to 75 pounds.

IRISH SETTER Some people consider the Irish Setter, with his lithe form and his rich mahogany color, the most beautiful of dogs. It is probable that he was developed from the English Setter, Irish Water Spaniel, and Pointer, with perhaps some Gordon Setter blood. He is a high-class gun dog on all kinds of game. His beauty, gaiety, courage, and personality have made him an ideal show dog and at times his great ability as a field dog has been neglected. A typical Irishman with a debonair personality, he is also bold but affectionate, tough and an excellent worker in the brush. Once he is trained on birds, he is trained for life. Height usually about 27 inches at shoulder, weight around 70 pounds.

English Setter

Gordon Setter

Irish Setter

Irish Setter and Pups

SPORTING DOGS

AMERICAN WATER SPANIEL   It is in the Middle West of the United States that the true American Water Spaniel has remained true to type. His coat, conformation, and color suggest the Irish Water Spaniel, English Water Spaniel, and Curly-Coated Retriever. He has been bred as a true working gun dog and has an excellent nose. He works fast and with zest in the field and does not stop until every bird or rabbit is brought in, treating each of them with gentleness. He swims like a seal, with his tail acting as a rudder in rough water. He springs game rather than pointing it. Solid liver or dark chocolate in color, the coat should be closely curled and dense for protection in cold water. Height 15 to 18 inches, weight 25 to 45 pounds.

BRITTANY SPANIEL   This dog originally came from France and has been in existence for centuries. Although called a Spaniel, he is similar to a Setter in size and working manners. Liver and white, or preferably orange and white, with short tail or none, Brittany Spaniels are excellent gun dogs and good retrievers. They are often field trial winners. The coat, which is somewhat wavy, should be close to the body. Height 17½ to 20½ inches, weight 30 to 40 pounds.

Brittany Spaniel

American Water Spaniel

CLUMBER SPANIEL The Clumber Spaniel's long, low body indicates Basset Hound blood, and the head which is heavy with a definite haw or droop of the lower eyelid probably comes as a result of old Alpine Spaniel ancestors. His name came from Clumber Park, the estate of the Duke of Newcastle in Nottingham, England. This dog works slowly but with dignified sureness and is an excellent retriever when well-trained. His chief characteristics are his low-slung body and his lemon-and-white coloring, preferably with few markings. Weight ranges from 35 to 65 pounds.

COCKER SPANIEL An ancient breed, the Spanyell was mentioned in an English document as early as 1386. There were two sizes. The smaller became the English Toy Spaniel, while the larger became the Cocker (he was excellent at work with woodcock) and was and still is a sporting dog. Today, the Cocker is the smallest dog of the sporting group. Due to his great desire to hunt, he is an excellent gun dog. Generally he quarters the ground ahead of the gun. After flushing game, he should stop or drop to a sitting position and retrieve only on command. A good swimmer, he is excellent at water retrieving. He makes a most companionable pet and is a home and family lover. He is gentle with children and enjoys romping with them. The colors have become a prime factor in the classification of the breed today: solid black, red, cream, buff, or liver; parti-colored black and white, black and tan, and red and white; or tricolors black, tan, and white, with markings in definite locations preferred. Black and tan come under ASCOB (any solid color other than black.) Each has its own group in judging. Height at withers should be 14 to 15½ inches, no more.

Clumber Spaniel

ASCOB Black and Tan Cocker Spaniel

Cocker Spaniel

Head of Cocker Spaniel

Parti-Colored Cocker Spaniel

ASCOB Black and Tan Cocker Spaniel

Cocker Spaniel Puppies

SPORTING DOGS

English Cocker Spaniel

English Springer Spaniel

Head of English Springer Spaniel

ENGLISH COCKER SPANIEL   The Cocker Spaniel descended from the original Spaniels of Spain, and the dogs became variable in size. The larger ones hunted game and the smaller ones woodcock. In the Kennel Club of England in 1892 the name English Cocker Spaniel was given to the dog that hunted woodcock. The breed is attractive, gay, and active, with short body and strong limbs. The head formation is peculiar to it alone, indicating great intelligence and in perfect symmetry with the body. The dog shows great love and faithfulness to his human family and is a ready worker both in the field and as a companion. Height 15 to 17 inches at withers, weight 26 to 34 pounds.

ENGLISH SPRINGER SPANIEL   This breed is a medium-sized sporting dog with compact body and docked tail. He is well proportioned and has a proud, erect carriage. The English Springer has balance and great style and zest, is friendly and anxious to please. His Spaniel characteristics should be strong. The coat should be flat or wavy and thick enough to be weatherproof. It may be liver or black with white markings, liver and white or black and white with tan markings, blue or liver roan or white with tan, black, or liver markings. Height 19 to 20 inches, weight about 49 to 55 pounds.

FIELD SPANIEL   The Field Spaniel is a result of the crosses of the Welsh Cocker and the Sussex Spaniel and later Springer and Cocker crossbreeding. He is usually black, liver, mahogany red, or roan in color, and has become an excellent field dog. He has intelligence, endurance, agility, and great perseverance. Height about 18 inches to shoulder, weight 35 to 50 pounds.

IRISH WATER SPANIEL   This breed originated centuries ago when there were land and water Spaniels, and was developed in Ireland. The tallest of the Spaniels, the Irish Water Spaniel is the clown of the family, with his very curly topknot between his eyes. He is loyal to his family but wary of strangers. The distinctive characteristics are the coat and tail. Tight crisp ringlets, not woolly, should cover his neck, back, and sides. He is solid liver color. His characteristic "rat tail" is thick at the root, with short curls there, then it tapers smoothly to the end. He is a great water dog, a good swimmer, and his coat sheds water. Height 21 to 24 inches, weight 45 to 65 pounds.

SUSSEX SPANIEL   The Sussex got its name from having been bred in Sussex, England, by a Mr. Fuller who developed the breed with the characteristic rich golden liver color. With superb nose, the Sussex is a determined hunter and outstanding for upland shooting. Perhaps because he is slower in movement than some other Spaniels, he is not so well known in America. Weight 35 to 45 pounds.

Field Spaniel

Irish Water Spaniel

Sussex Spaniel

WELSH SPRINGER SPANIEL   The Welsh Springer has been found mostly in Wales where he has been known for several hundred years. Because of his tolerance to extremes of heat and cold, he is now being used in many countries with varying climates, including the United States, Thailand, and Australia. He has a flat and even outercoat with soft undercoat—always red and white. He is a good water dog and works faithfully and willingly with any sort of game. This dog is a true friend and a good guard dog, and he loves children. He can live in the city and be happy, but he really is a vigorous country dog at heart. In size he comes between the Cocker and the English Springer.

Welsh Springer Spaniel

Welsh Springer Pup

SPORTING DOGS

Vizsla

VIZSLA This dog is really the Hungarian Pointer and dates back at least a thousand years. A dog like the Vizsla appears in tenth century stone carvings of a Magyar huntsman with his falcon. Between World War I and II the Vizsla became almost extinct, but as Hungarians fled before the Russian invasion of 1945 they took their dogs with them to Austria and other countries. The breed was admitted to the American Kennel Club registry in 1960. It is Pointer in type, with a proud bearing and a short rusty-gold coat and docked tail. Lean and powerful, the Vizsla is excellent for work on game birds, rabbits, and waterfowl and is an affectionate companion in the home. Height 22 to 24 inches at shoulder, weight 45 to 60 pounds.

Weimaraner

WEIMARANER　With the Bloodhound and the German Shorthaired Pointer among its ancestors, the Weimaraner dates back only to the early nineteenth century. The breed was promoted by the sporting members of the Weimar court in Germany to work with big game like wolves and bears. Then large wild game became rare and the dog was trained for smaller quarry. It was not easy to buy a Weimaraner and none were exported. There were never more than fifteen hundred in Germany. According to the strict breeding rules if a puppy was not to specification, it had to be destroyed. The breed was introduced to this country in 1929. The Weimaraner's coat is a distinctive color, silver or mouse gray. His eyes are amber, gray, or blue-gray, but appear black under excitement. He likes to be a real member of the family. Height at withers 23 to 27 inches.

Afghan Hound

Afghan Hound Head Study

AFGHAN HOUND   The Afghan's history can be traced back to 3000 or 4000 B.C. to the mountains where Moses received the Ten Commandments. He lived as royalty in the Egyptian court and with the desert sheiks and had great value as a hunting dog. Because of his black mask he was often called "monkey face." Later the breed was established in the northern part of Afghanistan and became a great favorite because of its ability to hunt leopard as well as smaller and less dangerous game. The thick, silky coat is very fine in texture and gives the Afghan built-in insulation. The tail carriage is high, thus enabling the hunter to see the dog in high thickets. The hipbones are another distinctive feature, higher and much wider apart than in most dogs. Thus the Afghan can run and jump over uneven ground and turn easily. He is an aloof and dignified dog and very much an aristocrat. The breed is becoming quite popular today. These dogs are delightful companions. They are real eye-catchers with their silky coats in cream, dark brindle, or black, black masks, furry legs, and long swinging ears. Height 25 to 27 inches, weight 50 to 60 pounds.

BASENJI   This is the "barkless" dog who when he is happy makes an infectiously gay sound between chortle and yodel. The history of Basenjis dates back to the days when they were brought from Central Africa as presents to the Pharaohs of ancient Egypt. The Basenji is the size and build of a Fox Terrier. He is used for pointing and retrieving. The texture of his coat is very fine and glossy, and he is fastidious, washing himself like a cat. Eager to please and gentle as a kitten, he is obedient and lively, fond of children, and possessed of boundless energy. His pointed ears and bright eyes give him a look of great intelligence and attentiveness. The white-tipped tail is tightly curled and lies over to one side of the back. Height 17 inches at shoulder, weight 22 to 24 pounds.

BASSET HOUND   This is an old breed of dog aristocrats, flourishing in France and Belgium where royalty bred it and used it for the slow trailing of deer, hares, and other game. It is descended from the old French Bloodhound and the St. Hubert Hound. Bassets are excellent in hunting in thick cover because of their short legs. In this country they are used to trail and flush and secure wounded pheasants and other game birds. With the skull peak highly developed, the breed is intelligent and docile, with a good disposition. The long soft ears and sad, deeply sunken eyes are characteristic. Height 11 to 15 inches at shoulder, weight from 25 to 40 pounds.

Basenji

Basset Hound Close Up

Basset Hound

15-inch Beagle

13-inch Beagle

Beagle Puppy

Bloodhound

BEAGLE   This is one of the oldest breeds, dating back to the days of ancient Greece. In the middle of the nineteenth century in Essex, England, a good pack, the beginning of the modern Beagle, was formed by the Reverend Philip Honeywood. Any true Hound color is satisfactory in the breed. The dog should look rather like a smaller Foxhound. He is excellent at hunting rabbits and hares. Big-boned and solid for his small size, he makes a lively and jaunty house dog and likes children. There are two groups of these Hounds, one 13 to 15 inches in height, the other under 13 inches.

BLOODHOUND   Back in the third century A.D. this Hound was mentioned, along with its peculiarly great ability to follow the faintest scent. The black Bloodhounds were the famous St. Huberts of the eighth century. In the twelfth century church dignitaries bred these Hounds, keeping the strain clean and calling the patrician dogs "blooded Hounds." Further development took place in the United States. The purebred Bloodhound is friendly and docile. He trails mostly for his own sport and does not attack the person he is trailing. Because of the accuracy of scent he can follow a person many miles and is the only dog whose evidence a court of law will accept. His long, sad, lined face and drooping ears are typical —he almost looks like a dignified judge himself. Colors are mostly black and tan, tawny, or red and tan. Height 24 to 26 inches, weight 80 to 100 pounds.

Bloodhound Head

BORZOI   Formerly known here as the Russian Wolfhound, the Borzoi has been a hunter in Russia for several centuries. The crossing of Arabian Greyhounds and a native Russian breed similar to the Collie created the elegant and graceful Borzoi of today. The dogs have a heavy, wavy or curly coat, usually with white predominating, and a long gracefully curved tail. The long legs indicate extreme speed. Borzois have great courage and are lithe and aristocratic. Height at shoulder 28 to 31 inches, weight 75 to 105 pounds.

BLACK AND TAN COONHOUND   Ancestors of the Coonhound were known in eleventh century England. With selective breeding for color the black and tan was developed through the years. This dog is outstanding for hunting opossum and raccoon. He hunts entirely with nose to ground and when he has treed his quarry he barks loudly. A working dog with tolerance to heat, cold, and

difficult country, his appearance suggests power and aggressiveness but he is also friendly. Height 23 to 27 inches at shoulder.

DACHSHUND   Dachshund in German means badger dog. The breed's history dates to fifteenth century Germany where these streamlined dogs were used to hunt badgers and rabbits. Early in the seventeenth century the smooth and long-haired varieties prevailed but in 1890 wirehairs were added. Robust and compact, the Dachshund should give no impression of awkwardness. Today these dogs are seldom used in the United States for hunting but are very popular as pets. They are affectionate and responsive companions with many humorous antics. They are odorless, do not shed hair, and require very little care. The three coat varieties appear in the standard size and also in the miniature, with weight under 9 pounds. The predominating colors are solid red or black and tan.

Borzoi

Black and Tan Coonhound

Dachshunds

Smooth-Coated Dachshund

Wirehaired Dachshund

Longhaired Dachshund

Miniature Dachshund

Dachshund Pup

HOUNDS

Scottish Deerhound

American Foxhound

English Foxhound

SCOTTISH DEERHOUND This breed was known as early as the sixteenth century as the Deerhound and was used, as the name implies, with deer in the highlands of Scotland. It also has been used to hunt wolves, coyotes, and rabbits. The Deerhound has a keen scent and great speed, is very tractable, and is loyal and devoted to his master. He should resemble a larger, rough-coated Greyhound. Dark gray is most preferred—the less white he shows, the better. Height 28 to 32 inches at shoulder, weight 75 to 110 pounds.

AMERICAN FOXHOUND In 1650 Robert Brooke arrived in Virginia from England with his pack of Hounds. From these dogs the American Foxhound developed. In America the breed is used as a field trial Hound or individually or in packs of about twenty or more for hunting fox. The general impression should be one of strength and action, the eyes gentle and soft. Chest, shoulders, legs, and feet count high in judging. There are wide variations of color. Height at shoulder 21 to 25 inches.

ENGLISH FOXHOUND There is little real reason for the word English in this breed's name, since foxhunting with Hounds has been practiced in this country almost as long as in England. The breeding of Foxhounds began well before 1800 and has always been in the hands of the masters of Hounds who kept very careful records. The English Foxhound has a sturdier frame than the American Foxhound. One admirer compared the Foxhound's symmetry to an ancient Greek statue for grace and strength. Color varies widely and is far less important than conformation in judging. There are over one hundred packs of English Foxhounds in America. Height 23 inches at shoulder.

GREYHOUND The Greyhound was first seen in Egypt, but now he lives in every country in the world. He has always been a symbol of aristocracy, and the description "swift as a ray of light, graceful as a swallow" fits him perfectly. The Greyhound is shown in tomb paintings of the Nile Valley dating back to about 3000 B.C., and he obviously belonged to royalty. In early English law "no meane person" might keep Greyhounds. The name probably came from the prevailing color in the breed. Long and lean, with smooth coat and patrician shape, the Greyhound has for many years been an emblem of speed. Within recent decades he has become a great racing dog, coursing the mechanical "rabbit" that is used on circular or oval tracks. Weight 60 to 70 pounds.

HARRIER It is believed that the Harrier was brought to England by the Normans. The first pack of Harriers in England was gathered in 1260. Hare hunting was always a sport there and these packs could be followed on foot. There have been Harriers in America since colonial days. The Harrier of today is a small edition of the Foxhound. Some have a distinctive blue mottle color, but most are in Foxhound colors. Height 19 to 21 inches at shoulder.

Greyhound

Harrier

Irish Wolfhound

Norwegian Elkhound

IRISH WOLFHOUND   This largest of all dogs was well known in Roman days. He is used to hunt wild boar in Europe, lions in Africa, coyotes, brush wolves, and timber wolves in America. He is a large Hound with rough coat, bright eyes, and shaggy brows. A tireless runner of power and speed, he moves with ease. In spite of his great size he has a peaceable disposition. He makes a good companion, even-mannered and dignified. Height 30 to 32 inches at shoulder, weight 105 to 120 pounds.

NORWEGIAN ELKHOUND   The Norwegian Elkhound comes from very early Viking days. A hunter of big game including elk, he tracks by instinct and intuition and can take a scent from two or three miles. He is now expert on lynx and mountain lion or smaller quarry. A compact medium-sized dog, he has a thick rich gray coat with soft undercoat, and he carries his tail curled tightly over his back. Today the popularity of the breed is based on friendliness and intelligence, his dependability, sensitivity, and boldness. Height 18 to 20½ inches at shoulder.

OTTER HOUND   A good deal of mystery surrounds the origin of the Otter Hound. In England otters preyed on fish in the rivers, and otter hunting has been carried on there for centuries. In the nineteenth century many packs of Otter Hounds hunted regularly through the season. The Otter Hound is an expert swimmer, helped by his webbed feet. He is a great worker and devoted to his master. In appearance he is similar to the Bloodhound except for his coat, which is hard, crisp, and oily, and for the most part keeps his body dry in the water. The color is grizzled, blue and white, or different shades of black and tan. Height 24 to 26 inches, weight about 65 pounds.

RHODESIAN RIDGEBACK   This dog is a native of South Africa and often called the African Lion Hound. During the sixteenth and seventeenth centuries the Dutch and Germans brought Mastiffs and Greyhounds, Bloodhounds and Terriers with them to South Africa. A half-wild hunting dog native to Africa crossbred with some of these European immigrants to establish the present Ridgeback. The unique feature, inherited from its wild African ancestors, is the ridge along the back where the hair grows in the opposite direction from the rest of the coat. The ridge should be definite, tapering, and symmetrical, starting behind the shoulders and continuing to the hips. Color is wheat, light to red. This dog is becoming a favorite in America. He is clean, never noisy or quarrelsome, loves children, and has a great desire to please. Height 24 to 27 inches at shoulder, weight 65 to 75 pounds.

SALUKI   This is the oldest known breed of dog; carvings of a dog very much like the Saluki were found in tombs of the Sumerian empire dating 7000 to 6000 B.C. He was the royal dog of Egypt, and his mummified body was often buried with the Pharaohs. When the word *dog* appears in the Bible, it means Saluki. The Saluki has a Greyhound body, with feathered ears, tail, and legs (a smooth variety lacks the feathering). Due to his great speed he was used by the Arabs to bring down the swift gazelle. He hunts mostly by sight, that sense being extraordinarily keen. This dog is graceful and aristocratic and has great symmetry, especially when running. Being both highly decorative and gentle, he makes an appealing companion. Height 23 inches or under to 28 inches.

Otter Hound

Rhodesian Ridgeback

Saluki

WHIPPET This breed is similar to a miniature Greyhound. The Whippet is a sporting dog, mainly a racer, making a speed up to 35 miles per hour. He is also a rabbit courser. A relatively new dog, he was first bred in England about a hundred years ago. The early crossings were small English Greyhounds and various Terriers, but later Italian Greyhound blood improved the type. Whippet racing became and remains a great sport in England and is now popular here, especially along the East Coast. The dog has a very alert appearance and should be in hard condition, lithe and muscular. Ideal height, 18 to 22 inches, weight around 20 pounds.

Whippet

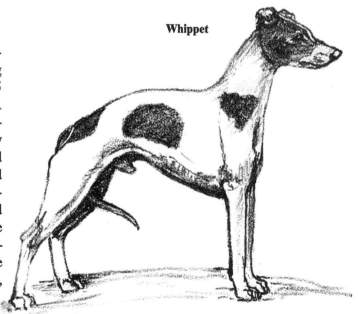

WORKING DOGS

Alaskan Malamute

ALASKAN MALAMUTE   This breed is one of the oldest of the Arctic sled dogs, named after the tribe called Mahlemuts who lived in the upper western part of Alaska. The tribal name was later changed to Malamute, and as the people were never without their dogs, the dogs too were called Malamute. These dogs traveled hundreds of miles with sledges and were better cared for than most other Arctic dogs. Although powerful and substantial, they are affectionate and friendly, active and alert. Today the Malamute has become popular as a sled dog for fun, and there are many teams of these beautiful creatures. Usually their heavy coats are gray or black and white. Their furry tails are carried over the back when they are not at work. The dogs like people, especially children. Height 22 to 25 inches, weight 75 to 85 pounds.

BELGIAN SHEEPDOG   As it is known today this breed was developed at the end of the nineteenth century in Belgium. The Belgium Kennel Club recognized the black long-haired sheepdogs and the Royal Society of St. Hubert gave them championships. The Groenendael, named for the village of its development and imported by breeders to America in

1907, has become very popular. They are gleaming black, some with limited white markings. They are devoted companions, sometimes even possessive, and good workers with vast energy. During World War I thousands were trained as messengers between the lines. Height 22 to 26 inches.

BELGIAN TERVUREN   This dog resembles the Groenendael or Belgian Sheepdog in conformation but differs in color. It was bred to type in the town of Tervuren, Belgium. The hair of the Tervuren is harsh and at the puppy stage it is light fawn, but as the dog grows older it becomes mahogany color overlaid with black. Only the tips of the hairs are black, extending over the dog like a veil. This dog is very deft at obedience work. He is intelligent, alert, courageous, and devoted to his master. Height 22 to 26 inches.

BERNESE MOUNTAIN DOG   This breed was brought to Switzerland two thousand years ago by Roman soldiers. The dogs have been used by the weavers of Berne to draw small wagons loaded with baskets to the market. The Bernese is handsome and aristocratic, with long black hair, brown or tan markings, and a brilliant white chest. White feet, tail-tip, and forehead blaze add to his distinctiveness. He is wise, hardy, and faithful. Height at shoulder 21 to 27½ inches.

Belgian Sheepdog

Belgian Tervuren

Bernese Mountain Dog

Bouvier des Flandres

BOUVIER DES FLANDRES   The Bouvier was first seen in southwest Flanders and the northern French hills, a working dog expert at herding cattle. In Belgium a Bouvier must win a prize in work competition as a defense, police, or army dog before he can win a championship. He is a rough-coated rugged dog with bushy eyebrows. His color varies from fawn to black or he may be salt-and-pepper or brindle. Powerfully built, he stands foursquare and has an intelligent expression. During World War I he was both ambulance and messenger dog. Height 23 to 27½ inches.

BOXER   Although the Boxer was known in the sixteenth century, it reached its perfection in Germany within the past hundred years. It is related to all breeds of the Bulldog type; these go back to the basic Molossus or Mastiff of Tibet which produced the fawn color. The Boxer also has some terrier blood. Used for bull baiting until it was outlawed, the Boxer now often does police work. As a policeman he must be intelligent, fearless, agile, and strong. He is also devoted to his master. His name comes from his manner of fighting which he begins with his front paws. The colors are solid fawn or brindle, often with white markings, and a black mask is required. Height 21 to 24 inches at shoulder.

Boxer

Boxer Head Study

BRIARD   The Briard goes all the way back to the twelfth century in France. Formerly used as defense against wolves and robbers, these are now the chief sheepdogs of France. Strong and solid, they are not rapid learners but they have retentive memories. Besides being excellent guard and sheepdogs, they have good records as police and war dogs, doing much active carrying work. Height 22 to 27 inches at shoulder.

BULLMASTIFF   In the latter part of the nineteenth century in England Bulldogs and Mastiffs were crossed to produce special dogs to protect large estates from poachers. In the resulting breed the light fawn color appeared and the black mask was inherited from the Mastiff. Other colors are brindle and red. Today these fearless, strong, active dogs are used as guards and protect their human families with great boldness and loyalty. Height 24 to 27 inches at shoulder, weight 100 to 130 pounds.

Boxer Teenagers

Briard

Smooth Collie

Bullmastiff

WORKING DOGS

COLLIE This breed has two varieties—rough-coated and smooth. Rough Collies date back to 1700 in Scotland and have always been associated with sheepherding. The Smooth Collie was a drover's dog who guided sheep and cattle to the marketplace. When Queen Victoria first visited Balmoral Castle, she saw the Rough Collies and immediately took a fancy to them, thus making them famous. The name Collie came from "coally dogs," so-called because of the black in the coats of early specimens. One of the first pure-bred dogs imported to this country, the Collie, especially the rough-coated, has retained great popularity. Beautifully proportioned and lithe, the head is especially important and should be lean and wedge-shaped. Colors are sable and white, tricolor, blue merle, and white. The Smooth is judged by the same standard as the Rough, but his coat must be hard and dense. Height 22 to 26 inches at shoulder, weight 60 to 75 pounds.

Collie

Collie Head Study

DOBERMAN PINSCHER   This dog, named for Louis Doberman, was bred about 1890 in Apolda, Germany, a cross of old shepherd dog with Rottweiler, Black and Tan Terrier, and smooth-haired German Pinscher. He is a true blue blood, lean, stripped ready for action, elegant in carriage. He is obedient and loyal to his master but judges a stranger with great care. Devoted to his home, he was at first a guard dog, later becoming a war and police dog. Colors are black, brown, and blue, sometimes with markings. Height 24 to 28 inches at shoulder.

Doberman Pinscher

GERMAN SHEPHERD DOG   Evolved from old stock of herding and farm dogs the German Shepherd has always been a worker. Noted for loyalty and courage, he has been developed temperamentally and structurally through breeding and specialized training for which he is highly apt. He has a fine war and police record. As a leader of the blind he shows great intelligence and judgment, patience, and watchfulness. He makes an excellent protector and friend. Ideal height 23 to 25 inches at shoulder, weight 60 to 85 pounds.

German Shepherd Dog

Head of a German Shepherd

German Shepherd Pups

GIANT SCHNAUZER   The Schnauzer was brought to perfection of physical conformation and keen mental development in Germany, where he herded and drove cattle and other livestock. There are three sizes, the Giant, the Standard and the Miniature. The Standard is the oldest. He was crossed with smooth-coated dogs and later with rough-haired sheepdogs and the black Great Dane. The resulting high-spirited Giant has often served as an efficient guard at German breweries. Police work is now his main occupation. Colors are pure black, black with tan, and pepper and salt mixtures. With keen intelligence and upright stance, he deserves more popularity here than he has yet enjoyed. Height 21½ to 25½ inches at shoulder.

GREAT DANE   Of German origin in spite of his name, the Great Dane has blood of the Irish Wolfhound and the old English Mastiff in his veins. He has been known for over four hundred years. The Germans used the splendid animal as a boar Hound and indeed bred him for the purpose. This dog has size and weight, chiseled elegance, speed, endurance, and courage. He makes a fine guard and companion, friendly and dependable. His glossy short coat comes in many colors: brindle, fawn, blue, black, and harlequin. His lean beauty and great size make him a real eye-catcher. Height 28 to over 30 inches at shoulder.

GREAT PYRENEES   This is the dog of French royalty and nobility as well as the friend and helper of the peasant shepherds of the Pyrenees. He dates back to antiquity, a descendant of the Mastiff type depicted in Babylonian art, whose remains were found around the Baltic and North Sea coasts. In 1675 the young French Dauphin saw one of these dogs and took it back to the royal palace. The breed immediately became the favorite of nobility. But on the lonely Pyrenees slopes, the great dog was guardian of the flocks and showed devotion and intelligence to both man and beast. He could attack and kill wolves and bears. In 1824 General Lafayette brought the first pair to a friend in America. The immense, serious, and gentle Great Pyrenees is excellent for pulling carts and for pack and guide work on ski trips. The predominating color is white: he has been called "an animated snowdrift." Height at shoulder 25 to 32 inches, weight 90 to 125 pounds.

Giant Schnauzer

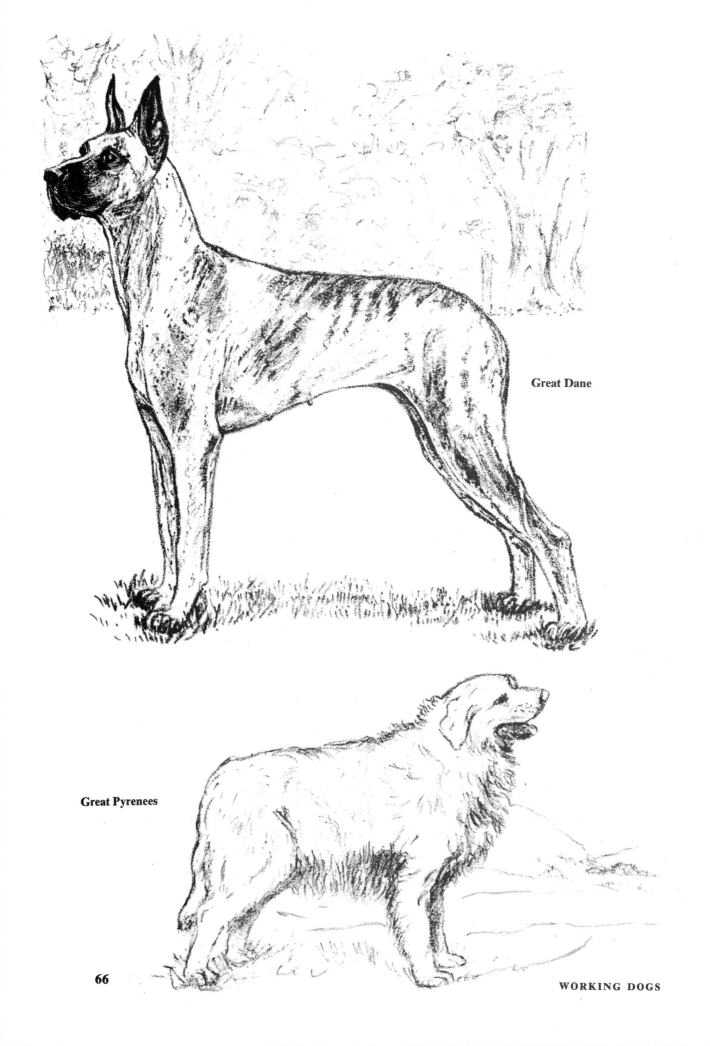

Great Dane

Great Pyrenees

Komondor

Kuvasz

Mastiff

KOMONDOR   The Magyars of Hungary have bred Komondorok, the plural of Komondor, for over a thousand years. The dogs have great courage and are thoroughly trustworthy, the protectors (more the overseers than the herders) of huge flocks of sheep. The Komondor is a powerful dog with strong bones, a staunch defender of his own against strangers. His shaggy coat, which even covers his face, should not be too curly. The hair must be white. Height 28 to 30 inches at shoulder.

KUVASZ   Originally from high, far-off Tibet, the Kuvasz was developed in Hungary also. In some countries of medieval Europe only royal favorites were allowed to own Kuvaszok (the plural). At first a palace guard dog, the Kuvasz later became a guardian of sheep and cattle. The name comes from a Turkish word meaning "armed guard of the nobility." With lightness of movement in spite of his size, the Kuvasz is impressively strong and active. His coat should be pure white and quite thick, his nose black. Height at shoulder about 26 inches or less.

MASTIFF   The Mastiff has been bred as a watchdog in England for over two thousand years. The real name is Old English Mastiff. Caesar described these dogs in his invasion of Britain in 55 B.C., when they fought valiantly along with their masters against the Romans. Some were taken to Rome where they fought victoriously at the circus. There have been in literature many heroic tales of the Mastiff since those days. This dog is a combination of courage and good nature, massive and well-knit and

docile. Body color varies but the darker the better for muzzle, eyes, and ears. Height at shoulder about 26 inches.

NEWFOUNDLAND   Definitely a native of Newfoundland this dog is thought to be descended from Great Pyrenees dogs brought over by Basque fishermen. Later the breed was perfected in England. The Newfoundland was a real lifesaver, swimming far to rescue people from the sea, carrying lifelines to stricken vessels, saving children who fell into the water and bringing them ashore. He is also used for pulling carts and carrying burdens and he takes on the duties of nursemaid to children naturally. His coat is heavy and jet black. Intelligence, loyalty, and sweetness are predominating traits. Height 26 to 28 inches at shoulder, weight 110 to 150 pounds.

OLD ENGLISH SHEEPDOG   The ancestry of this dog can be traced back 150 years. Some people say he is a cross of the Scotch bearded Collie and the Russian Owtchar. In early days he was a drover's dog. Such dogs were tax-exempt and their tails were docked to prove their occupation, hence the nicknames "bob" and "bobtail." They are born with very short tails but show dogs today have the tail completely removed. Because of their intelligence, love for home, agility, and affection, they make ideal house dogs and can also be trained as retrievers. The shaggy coat serves as insulation against both cold and heat. At slow pace they have a shuffling, bear-like gait. Color should be generally gray or grizzled with white. Height about 20 to 22 inches.

Newfoundland

Old English Sheepdog

Puli

PULI The Puli (plural Pulik) has been in Hungary for over a thousand years and is a great sheepdog. There is probably Tibetan Terrier in his background. Hungarian shepherds used him as drover and as guard. The color is usually weathered black, often tinged with bronze, sometimes gray or white. The coat of the Puli is most unusual. The undercoat is soft and woolly, the outercoat long and dense. As the dog grows to maturity, the two coats intertangle and he looks bigger than he really is. In this country he is kept groomed. Vigorous, alert, very active and affectionate, he makes an excellent and distinctive-looking guard dog. Height about 17 inches, weight about 30 pounds.

Rottweiler

ROTTWEILER The Rottweiler is descended from Roman cattle dogs and gets his name from the town of Rottweil in Württemberg, south Germany. The early expeditions of the Romans across the Alps and into Central Europe necessitated the moving of large herds of cattle along with the armies, and good drover dogs went along. Later the butchers of Rottweil needed dogs that would be good workers, trusted companions, and reliable guards. From 1910 the Rottweiler has been used for police training. He is a dignified, obedient dog with great courage, modesty, and self-reliance. His coarse black coat is short and has tan or brown markings. Height 22 to 27 inches at shoulder.

ST. BERNARD Dogs were probably introduced at the ancient Hospice of St. Bernard in the Swiss Alps about 1665. As the monks took the dogs along with them on trips of mercy, they discovered that they were excellent pathfinders in the deep snows and were very apt at finding lost travelers. Traveling in groups, two of the dogs would lie beside a freezing traveler to keep him warm, licking his face to revive him. Another would hasten back to give the alarm to the Hospice. These dogs have been responsible for saving many hundreds of lives. They required no special training; their rescuing instinct is inherent, as is their ability to detect an avalanche in advance. Gentle and devoted to service, these great dogs have a highly intelligent expression. They are a hardy breed, and their heavy coats make them ideally suited to withstand severe cold. Generally they are white and red. Height 25½ to 27½ inches at shoulder.

SAMOYED The Samoyeds were very primitive people living on the tundra area of ice and snow near the White Sea. They depended for life on their reindeer herd and on their dogs which served as shepherds, sledge dogs, and companions. The Samoyed dog has bred true all the centuries, with no fox or wolf in the strain. He is the modern breed nearest the primitive dog. His constant companionship with man through centuries has given him an almost human understanding, with a happy, childlike attitude. The great Arctic and Antarctic expeditions have used these dogs because of their reliability, courage, and faithfulness. The white dog has great gaiety and joyousness and seems to smile. His heavy double coat is white or nearly white and includes a ruff around the neck. Height 19 to 23½ inches at withers.

STANDARD SCHNAUZER This German breed has been loved by artists for centuries and is seen in portraits by Dürer, Rembrandt, Lucas Cranach the Elder, and Sir Joshua Reynolds. The Schnauzer is the result of the crossing of the black German Poodle, gray wolf Spitz, and wirehaired Pinscher stock. He is a yard dog, guard, and rat catcher. During the war Schnauzers were dispatch carriers and Red Cross aides, and they also did and still do police work. A four-square solid dog, his rugged build and harsh coat is usually pepper and salt, and his accent marks include bushy brows, mustache, and a luxuriant chin beard. Height at withers 17 to 20 inches.

SHETLAND SHEEPDOG A Collie in miniature, this dog comes from the Shetland Islands where all the local animals are bred small because subsistence is hard. These dogs are as old as the working Collie and today have all the points of type, expression, and symmetry of the Collie, together with the size, charm, and character which makes them a sort of cousin of the Shetland pony. They are excellent at farm work and as companions. Colors include black, blue merle, and from tan to mahogany in the browns. Height at shoulder 13 to 16 inches.

SIBERIAN HUSKY A native of northeastern Siberia properly called Siberian Chuchis, these dogs are used by the natives as guards, sled dogs, and companions for the children. Some of them were imported to Alaska for racing in the early nineteenth century and they now provide the power for sled-dog racing in Alaska, Canada, and the United States. The Husky is friendly and gentle, quick, alert, intelligent, and tractable. He has a soft, thick double coat and is clean and free from body odor. Color and markings vary widely—any are allowable. Height at shoulder 20 to 23½ inches, weight 35 to 60 pounds.

St. Bernard

Samoyed Brace

72

Shetland Sheepdog

Standard Schnauzer

Siberian Husky

Head of Siberian Husky

Sled. Racing

Husky Sled Team

Cardigan Welsh Corgi

CARDIGAN WELSH CORGI This is one of the oldest breeds in the British Isles, brought from Central Europe to Cardiganshire by the Celts about 1200 B.C. The Cardigan Corgi was a member of the same family that produced the Dachshund. His uses were varied but chiefly he was guard to children, game dog, and a nipper of the heels of cattle to keep them in the right pasture. His head with its prominent ears, his body, and even his expression are reminiscent of a fox. His hard-textured coat comes in almost any color but pure white. Height 12 inches at shoulder, weight 15 to 25 pounds.

PEMBROKE WELSH CORGI This breed goes back to the early twelfth century and comes from Pembrokeshire, Wales. It is quite distinct from the Cardigan Corgi, and the Pembroke's family background includes the Keeshond, Pomeranian, Samoyed, Chow Chow and others. Compared to the Cardigan the Pembroke is shorter in body with straighter and lighter boned legs and a coat of finer texture. The Cardigan's ears are rounded while the Pembroke's ears are pointed at the tip. The Cardigan has a long tail and the Pembroke a short one. The agreeable little Pembroke is a congenial fireside companion, affectionate but not overzealous, alert, and intelligent. Height 10 to 12 inches, weight 18 to 24 pounds.

Pembroke Welsh Corgi

TERRIERS

Airedale Terrier

AIREDALE TERRIER   The history of the Airedale is a bit vague. The extinct black and tan terrier is an ancestor of Irish, Fox, Welsh, and Airedale Terriers. These dogs all had agility, courage, and keen eyesight and hearing, but it was not until a crossing with the Otter Hound that keen nose and swimming ability were added. Airedales are used for big game hunting in Africa and elsewhere. They have done police duty and acted as dispatch carriers. As these dogs make excellent companions and guards, they are popular in all countries. In profile the Airedale's jaw is pronouncedly square. His thick, wiry coat should lie close. Generally he is tan with dark markings. Height about 23 inches at shoulder.

AUSTRALIAN TERRIER   This breed descends from the Australian Rough with probable later crossings with the Cairn, the Dandie Dinmont, the Irish Terrier, the Yorkshire, and the Skye. This is one of the smallest of the working Terriers, an affectionate little dog of great courage and spirit and an assured air. He is generally blue-black or silver-black with tan markings. Height 10 inches at shoulder, weight 12 to 14 pounds.

BEDLINGTON TERRIER   The Bedlington comes from Bedlington, Northumberland, in the mining area of England. No trouble-maker himself by nature, he fights to the death, rather belying his innocent, lamblike appearance with rounded head and high back legs. Tractable and good company, he developed into a pet because of his lovable nature. His action is springy and he gallops like a Greyhound. Colors are liver and blue, with blue predominant today. Height 15 to 16 inches at shoulder, weight 22 to 24 pounds.

BORDER TERRIER   From the Cheviot Hills between England and Scotland came the Border Terrier, a skilled and tireless fox hunter with weatherproof coat to withstand the cold rainy climate. His head is like that of an otter, but his temperament and personality are pure Terrier, game and good-tempered. He comes in red, grizzle or blue with tan, or wheat color. Weight 11½ to 15½ pounds.

BULL TERRIER   There are two varieties of Bull Terriers, the white and the colored. The breed began in the nineteenth century with the crossing of a Bulldog with a now extinct white English Terrier, with later crossing with Spanish Pointer. Used in early dog fighting the Bull Terrier developed great strength, agility, and courage. He was taught to defend himself and his master, but never to provoke a fight, thus earning the title "the white cavalier." Muscular and determined, he is also friendly and affectionate. The standard for the colored variety is the same as for the white, with brindle a popular color. Weight varies widely, from 25 to 60 pounds.

Australian Terrier

Bedlington Terrier

Border Terrier

Bull Terrier

Colored Bull Terrier

Cairn Terrier

CAIRN TERRIER   The old-time working Terrier of the Isle of Skye is an ancestor of this breed. Cairns are workers, catching foxes, otters, and other animals from rock ledges and cliffs in their native island. The sporting instincts and "varmint-killing" ability of the dogs made them favorites of both lairds' and crofters' households. This hardy little fellow, short and broad of head, comes in all colors except white. Darker ears, muzzle, and tail tip are desirable. Height about 9½ inches, longer in body than the Sealyham or Scottish Terrier. Weight is 12 to 16 pounds.

Dandie Dinmont Terrier

DANDIE DINMONT TERRIER   About 1700 the Dandie Dinmont Terrier was bred from a crossing of the rough native Terrier of the Cheviot Hills and other breeds. He was a hunter of otter and badger. Sir Walter Scott made the breed famous and gave it its name in his 1814 novel *Guy Mannering,* whose chief character was a farmer named Dandie Dinmont. The Dandie's soft top hair and pendulous ears are as typical as his determined bright-eyed air. He is a good intelligent guard and fond of children, an ideal dog for outdoors or a small apartment. There are two distinct color ranges, pepper and mustard, with varying shades in each and with lighter points and topknots. Height at shoulder 8 to 11 inches, weight 18 to 24 pounds.

Dandie Dinmont Head Study

Wirehaired Fox Terrier

Smooth Fox Terrier

Irish Terrier

Kerry Blue Terrier

82

TERRIERS

FOX TERRIER There are two varieties of this popular and well-known old English breed, the Smooth and the Wire. The two types probably sprang from quite different sources but were earlier interbred. Both should be friendly, gay, and sprightly. The coat of the Smooth should be smooth, flat, hard, and dense. The coat of the Wire should be broken and harder and more wiry. White predominates in each. Height about 15 inches at withers.

IRISH TERRIER This dog with his wiry red coat, alert and trim, with intelligent eyes and a saucy debonair way, is a true Terrier in type and character and at the same time a true Irishman. He resembles an old Irish Wolfhound in minature, both in appearance and in character. He is a born guardsman, a protector of children, and a real sportman. He will catch and kill woodchucks, rabbits, and other small game. A lover of water, he can be trained to retrieve in it as well as on land. He was a great worker in World War I. Height about 18 inches at shoulder.

KERRY BLUE TERRIER Kerry Blues came from Ireland in County Kerry, where they have been purebred for over a hundred years. A good hunter and herdsman, the Kerry is also a courageous guard and friend, and has been adopted as the national dog of the Irish Republic. His color is a uniform gray-blue, deep slate or lighter. Height 17½ to 19½ inches at shoulder, weight 33 to 40 pounds.

LAKELAND TERRIER This is one of the oldest working Terrier breeds, coming from the lake district of England. Formerly Lakelands were used to hunt sheep-raiding foxes, along with several hounds. They have great courage and will follow underground for long distances, one having burrowed twenty-three feet after an otter. The early ancestors of the Lakeland were similar to the Border Terrier. This is a lively, brave, attractive little dog with a quiet disposition. Weight 16 to 17 pounds.

MANCHESTER TERRIER Many years ago in the Manchester district of England were held contests of rat killing and rabbit chasing. To produce a dog skilled at both contests a Whippet and a dark brown Terrier were crossed. The resulting dog became a great success. Formerly known as the Black-and-Tan, the breed is now called Manchester. In 1959 two separate classifications were established, the Standard and the Toy. In the Standard the ears may be erect or button, and if cropped they are long and carried straight up. The Toy's ears are uncropped and are carried naturally erect. The color in both groups is jet black and rich mahogany tan. Both make intelligent pets and companions. The Manchester's Whippet blood shows in his roached back. Weight for Standard, over 12 pounds to 22 pounds; for Toy, under 12 pounds.

NORWICH TERRIER Norwiches, sometimes called Jones Terriers, are relatively recent dogs, introduced into England in 1880 and to the United States after World War I. They are small, rugged, and very game little fellows, tremendously active and excellent in hunting rabbits. They make ideal house dogs, loyal and amusing, and their coats do not collect dirt or need trimming. Colors are black, tan, red, or grizzle. Height at shoulder, 10 inches, weight 10 to 14 pounds.

Kerry Blue Terrier Head Study

Lakeland Terrier

84

TERRIERS

Manchester Terrier

Toy Manchester Terrier

Norwich Terrier

Miniature Schnauzer

Scottish Terrier

Sealyham Terrier

MINIATURE SCHNAUZER Small-sized Standard Schnauzers were crossed with Affenpinschers to produce the Miniature. Usually this attractive little dog is salt and pepper color, but solid black and black-and-tan also occur. He is good in town life and small quarters, hardy, active, intelligent, and fond of children. He is not an aggressive fighter and seldom wanders. Weight 12 to 15 pounds.

SCOTTISH TERRIER Some people say, without too much definite proof either way, that this keen, compact little dog is the most ancient of the Highland Terriers. At any rate the small, perky, friendly little Scottie has been beloved for many years, a good companion and lover of children. The color is black, steel or iron gray, brindle, or wheaten. Height 10 inches at shoulder, weight 18 to 22 pounds.

SEALYHAM TERRIER The Sealyham, from Wales, is a fairly recent development but is a popular breed. Excellent at following otter, fox, and other small animals, he has great gameness and enduring power. His coat is soft and dense underneath, with a hard and wiry topcoat, quite weatherproof. Color is usually all white, occasionally with light color on head and ears. Powerful and determined, the Sealyham can dig well and fight his prey under ground. Height at withers 10½ inches, weight 20 to 21 pounds.

SKYE TERRIER Four centuries ago the Skye Terrier was very much the way he is today, with flowing coat and hair over his eyes. He came from the Isle of Skye, off the coast of Scotland, and was long a fashionable pet of the nobility. He is alert, with great style and dignity, fearless, good-tempered, and loyal. He may be of almost any color, but regardless,

muzzle, ears, and tip of tail should be dark. Height at shoulder about 9½ inches.

STAFFORDSHIRE TERRIER A crossing of Bulldog, used for bull baiting, and one or more types of Terriers produced the Staffordshire sometimes called Pit Terrier. The heavier specimens have been used for breeding in this country, so that often an American Staffordshire may be ten pounds heavier than an English Staffordshire. Though years ago these dogs were used for fighting, today they can be very docile and tractable. They should give the impression of great activity and strength for their size and are intelligent, conscientious guardians. Height 17 to 19 inches at shoulder.

WELSH TERRIER A very old breed, the Welsh Terrier has been hunting small animals with great gameness in Wales for many years. He was formerly known as the Black-and-Tan Wirehaired Terrier, and his present color is the same. He is not a quarrelsome dog, in spite of his courage, and is well-mannered and easily handled. Height 15 inches or less at shoulder, weight 20 pounds.

WEST HIGHLAND WHITE TERRIER This breed, originating at Poltalloch, Scotland, probably came from the same stock as the other Terriers from Scotland. These small, chesty little dogs are delightful pets, fast and cunning on the hunt, but gay and light of heart as indoor companions. Hardy and determined, they need and ask for no pampering. They should be pure white in color, but in spite of this are not difficult to look after. Both pointed ears and pointed tail should be erect. By no means should they be considered white Scottish Terriers—the two are quite distinct breeds. Height 10 to 11 inches at withers.

Skye Terrier

Staffordshire Terrier

Welsh Terrier

West Highland White Terrier

88 TERRIERS

TOYS

Affenpinscher

AFFENPINSCHER   The Affenpinscher is of the same family as the Brussels Griffon and his breed dates back at least to the seventeenth century in Europe. He is known as the "monkey dog," the monkeyish expression deriving from a prominent chin, hair tuft, mustache, and bushy eyebrows. He is small but not delicate, a very alert, intelligent, and game little dog whose popularity is increasing. His coat must be harsh and wiry, often black but sometimes red, gray, or a mixture. Height 10¼ inches at shoulder, weight not over 7 to 8 pounds.

Longhaired Chihuahua

Smooth Chihuahua

CHIHUAHUA   The dogs that were owned by the Toltecs who lived in Mexico in the ninth century were called Techichi. It is from them that the Chihuahua came. His colors vary from pure white to jet black and include black and tan. The United States, which has done much to perfect the breed for symmetry and intelligence, prefers solid colors and a smooth coat, though the long-coated Chihuahua is increasing in popularity. Clannishness is an outstanding trait; the Chihuahua generally prefers his own kind and does not like other breeds of dogs. The dog should have great bright eyes, a domed skull, and large ears held erect. Weight 1 to 6 pounds, with 2 or 3 pounds preferred.

ENGLISH TOY SPANIEL   This breed originated in Japan and was taken from there to Spain and then to England. It was a favorite of Mary, Queen of Scots, and one of her pets refused to leave her when she went to the scaffold. There are several types and colors. The King Charles is black and tan. The Prince Charles is white, black, and tan. The Ruby is chestnut red. The Blenheim is chestnut red and white. These dogs, though mostly pets, have excellent sporting instincts and are good hunters. Selective breeding has reduced the weight to from 6 to 12 pounds.

English Toy Spaniel

BRUSSELS GRIFFON   The little Brussels Griffon is brimful of personality and makes friends wherever he goes. He is a bundle of good nature and sauciness from turned-up nose to tip of his gaily carried tail. The breed came from the German Affenpinscher and the Belgian street dog. Later crossing with Chinese Pug produced the smooth-coated type, the Brabancon. Still later the Ruby Spaniel was crossed, adding the odd facial expression and some characteristics of the present-day dog. The Brussels Griffon is a small, compact dog with gay carriage. Color is generally black or reddish brown or a combination. The coat of the rough-coated type should be harsh and wiry. Weight usually 8 to 10 pounds.

Brussels Griffon

Italian Greyhound

Japanese Spaniel

Maltese

ITALIAN GREYHOUND This is a small, slender edition of the English Greyhound, long a favorite of aristocracy and royalty, including Frederick the Great. It has great style and elegance in both form and movement, with its gracefully curved back and high step. The hair must be thin and glossy, in shades of red, mouse, fawn, blue, cream, and white. There are two classes, 8 pounds and under, and over 8 pounds.

JAPANESE SPANIEL These dogs originated in China centuries ago, and drawings of them have been found there in old temples and in early art. A Chinese emperor gave a pair to the emperor of Japan. They were long owned only by nobility. In 1853 Commodore Perry brought some of them from Japan and gave a pair to Queen Victoria. Eventually they came to America. Highly bred, dainty, and lively little dogs, Japanese Spaniels are stylish in movement with high steps and tail carried over the back. The heavy coat is straight and silky, usually in black and white or white with yellow or red markings and matching nose. The eyes are prominent. Two classes, 7 pounds and under, and over 7 pounds.

MALTESE This little dog has been an aristocrat for twenty-eight hundred years. The Greeks often erected tombs for the Maltese pets. At the time of the Apostle Paul the Ro-

man governor of Malta had a favorite Maltese named Issa whose superbly realistic portrait he had painted. As these tiny dogs have been pure-bred through the centuries, the household pets of people of wealth and culture, they are themselves refined and very clean, healthy, and lively though small. Maltese are Spaniels not Terriers. They are intelligent and affectionate and make excellent pets, especially for older people. The coat is pure white and straight, with a full length part from nose to root of tail. Weight not over 7 pounds, and the smaller the better.

MANCHESTER TERRIER (TOY) For description of Toy Manchester Terrier, see Manchester Terrier in Terrier Group.

PAPILLON The Papillon was known in the sixteenth century as the dwarf Spaniel and was often pictured in great paintings and tapestries. Mme de Pompadour and Marie Antoinette both had them as pets. With his large, erect, long-haired ears, set obliquely and moving the way a butterfly's wings do, the Papillon is aptly named. White with markings of other colors is general. A second type of Papillon has ears that droop altogether, and sometimes the two types occur in the same litter. This dainty little dog is intelligent, gentle, and jaunty, and makes an excellent pet. Height 11 inches or less at withers.

Papillon

Pekingese

PEKINGESE   In ancient China where it originated this dog was held sacred. The beautifully carved Foo dog idols in ivory, porcelain, and wood depict the Pekingese. Some were called Lion Dogs because of their appearance and manner. Some were called Sun Dogs due to their beautiful golden-red coats. The third group, Sleeve Dogs, were so small they were carried in the large sleeves of members of the imperial household. When the palace was looted by the British in 1860, four of the dogs were found hidden behind some draperies. One was presented to Queen Victoria, the others bred by Lord Hay and the Duke of Richmond. The Pekingese is very popular in America today. He is calm and good-tempered, has plenty of stamina, is easy to care for, and makes a delightful pet. He is bold and esteems himself highly. All colors are allowed. Weight not over 14 pounds.

Pekingese Head Study

Miniature Pinscher

Pomeranian

Black Pug

MINIATURE PINSCHER   This little dog is originally a native of Germany but has long been bred in Scandinavia as well. He is almost a small copy of the Doberman Pinscher, with the manner of a dog larger than he really is. He is a born watchdog, with lively personality, intelligence, and a special feeling for his owner and his home. The short coat requires little care to keep neat and clean. The colors are solid red or brown, and black and tan. Height not over 11 inches at withers.

POMERANIAN   Descendant of the sled dogs of the far north, this little fellow was probably bred down in size in Pomerania. The tiny dog is docile, sturdy, and lively, and makes a most enjoyable pet. The coat is of profuse stand-off hair, and the tail should be turned over the back, set high, and carried flat. The prominent colors are black, brown, red, orange, cream, and sable.

POODLE (TOY)   For description see Poodle in the Non-Sporting Group.

PUG   Like most dogs with short faces and tightly curled tails, the Pug came originally from China and was brought to England by traders of the Dutch East India Company. The black Pug can be traced back to the Japanese Pug which is similar to the present-day Toy Spaniel. Pugs are compact and squarish, clean, alert, and companionable, requiring a minimum of care. Color is silver or apricot-fawn, with muzzle or mask black. The tail should be tightly curled over the hip, and a double curl is perfection. Weight 14 to 18 pounds.

Pug

"Potential Champions"

Pug Pups

Silky Terrier

SILKY TERRIER A native of Australia, the Silky was formerly called the Sydney Silky in honor of that city. He is the result of Australian Terrier crossbred with Yorkshire Terrier. The Silky is a friendly, forceful little dog, curious and light-footed and, if allowed to be, an excellent ratter. His coat should be silky in texture, blue and tan in color. The V-shaped ears are jaunty. Height 9 to 10 inches, weight 8 to 10 pounds.

YORKSHIRE TERRIER The Yorkshire Terrier was first shown in Leeds, England, in 1861. It is closely related to the Skye Terrier and also has some Maltese and Dandie Dinmont Terrier blood. The coloring is dark steel blue from top of the head to root of the tail, with a rich tan on head and chest. The puppies are born black. The coat should be long and straight and hang down on each side of the body, parted the full length. As his coat has to be handled carefully, he seldom is allowed to romp outside and has become a somewhat pampered pet. Though tiny, this little fellow can be quite spirited because of the Terrier influence. Height at shoulder 9 to 10 inches, weight 3 to 5 pounds.

Yorkshire Terrier

NON-SPORTING DOGS

Boston Terrier

BOSTON TERRIER   One of the few real American breeds, the Boston Terrier is a cross between an English Bulldog and a white English Terrier. By careful, selective breeding and some inbreeding, a clean-cut dog with short head, soft dark eyes, and a body with the conformation of a Terrier has resulted. This dog has a pleasing disposition and is known as the "American Gentleman" among dogs. He is a good companion and house pet. The coloring is brindle with white markings, though black with white is permissible. Weight not over 25 pounds.

BULLDOG   Bulldogs originated in the British Isles. Used for bull baiting they were ferocious and had enormous courage. After 1835 dogfighting became illegal in England, and breeders worked on eliminating the ferocity and developing the dog's fine qualities. Now the Bull has become a fine physical specimen, kind and peaceable with liking for everyone, especially children. The body is massive and thick-set with front legs wide apart, giving an appearance of vitality and stability. The coat is short and flat, ideally brindle with white markings. Weight about 40 to 50 pounds.

Bulldog

Bulldog Close Up

NON-SPORTING DOGS

Chow Chow

Dalmatian

Dalmatian Pups   **NON-SPORTING DOGS**

CHOW CHOW   This breed is Chinese and dates back more than two thousand years. It is thought by some to be a crossing of the old Tibetan Mastiff and the Samoyed, and is the only breed in the world with a blue-black tongue. The Chow is lion-headed and compact, with a straight, stand-off coat of black or cinnamon or any clear solid color. He has an expression of dignity and a scowl. His tail is carried close to his back and has lighter shadings, and his gait is short and somewhat stiff.

DALMATIAN   The origin of the Dalmatian is uncertain, but it goes far back into history, and there has been little change of type and conformation. He is often called the Coach or Carriage Dog, or the Fire House Dog. He loves horses and to trot along under the rear or front axle of a horse-drawn vehicle as follower and guardian. An aristocrat, the Dalmatian is a quiet gentleman, a good road dog, with great speed and elegance of motion. In color he is like no other dog, with his black or brown spots on a short, sleek white coat. The spots should be round and distinct. Height 19 to 23 inches, weight 35 to 50 pounds.

FRENCH BULLDOG   Descendant of the English Bull, these dogs became popular in France about 1860. Two features of the breed are the bat ears and the skull which is flat between the ears while above the eyes it should be slightly domed. The French Bulldog should have a bright, alert look and always be ready for fun. He should be well-balanced and compact, with a roach back. His smooth coat is loose, giving him wrinkles at head and shoulders. He makes an excellent pet as he is always good-tempered and dependable. Weight 20 to 28 pounds.

KEESHOND   This is the national dog of Holland, named after Kees de Gyselaer, the eighteenth century patriot leader whose dog became the symbol of the patriots. The origin is Arctic or Subarctic, and the dog is closely related to the Pomeranian. Keeshonden are intelligent and very alert and make ideal companions. It was sheer personality which gave them such popularity in Holland. The thick, stand-off coat is wolf-gray and always looks clean and freshly brushed. The tips of the hair are black, the muzzle dark, the ruff, "trousers," and plumed tail lighter. Height 15 to 18 inches at withers.

LHASA APSO   As these small dogs are natives of a country with a climate varying from intense cold to great heat, they have strong and vigorous constitutions. They came originally from the sacred city of Lhasa in Tibet and were raised by the lamas. Two outstanding features are the heavy coat and the tail curled over the back. The gay little Lhaso Apso has never lost his ability for keen watchfulness or his hardy nature. He is easily trained and responds to kindness. He comes in many different colors, with gold or lion color preferred. Height 10 to 11½ inches at shoulder.

POODLE   Of all breeds the Poodle is considered one of the most intelligent, almost superhumanly so at times, and this makes them delightful and enchanting companions. Their true origin is a mystery, but they probably originated in Germany, and the English name was derived from the German word Pudel. The larger or Standards make excellent retrievers, companions, and obedience trial winners. The Miniature and Toy Poodles are excellent and fashionably elegant pets for the city dweller. All have great dignity combined with sprightliness and lightness of action. The natural long coat can be almost any solid color. The dogs are clipped in different traditional styles, each with definite specifications. Height: Standard over 15 inches, Miniature 10 to 15 inches, Toy under 10 inches, all at withers.

French Bulldog

Keeshond

NON-SPORTING DOGS

Lhasa Apso

Standard Poodle

NON-SPORTING DOGS

Poodle Clips The three sizes of Poodles, Standard, Miniature, and Toy, are one breed and all have a coat which lends itself to different hair styling. The top coat is profuse and the hair is wiry in texture and curled closely, while the undercoat is woolly and warm. The clipping of a Poodle's coat is a matter of the taste of the owner. But for the dog show ring, it must be either the Continental or English Saddle Clip for dogs over a year old. Dogs under one year of age can be entered in the show ring in the Puppy class with face, feet, and base of tail shaved and the rest of the coat left natural length.

In the Continental Clip, the hindquarters are shaved bare with rosettes on the hips. The English Saddle Clip leaves a short-clipped saddle or blanket of hair which covers the hindquarters. The beautiful long coat is left on from the last or third rib from the rear and the hindquarters are scissored closely forming a saddle. The dog's face, feet, and legs are clipped leaving pompoms, one on the front legs and two on each rear leg.

For the Royal Dutch Clip, the head is clipped smooth leaving a mustache and goatee. The ears are clipped leaving a short or long fringe, whichever is desired, at the bottom. The topknot is rounded to a ball. The chest, stomach, and back are clipped smooth, leaving the hairs long on all four legs about four inches above the elbows. As in all clips, the feet and base of tail are clipped. With the Royal Dutch Clip, colored jackets and collars, often studded with colored stones, can be worn. As the Poodle is a gay animal, this decoration adds to his charm. The dogs seem to like to be dressed up.

The Puppy or Utility Clip is neat and easy to care for. The face, feet, and tail are clipped and the rest of the coat cut down to about an inch of curly hair which easily forms ringlets.

Miniature Poodle

Show or English Saddle clip

Continental clip

Royal Dutch Clip

Kennel or Puppy clip

Poodle Clips

Silver Miniature Poodle Head Study

Black Miniature Poodle Head Study

Black Miniature Poodle Show Clip

NON-SPORTING DOGS

Toy Poodle

SCHIPPERKE   These faithful little watchdogs came from the Flemish provinces of Belgium. The name, pronounced Skip-per-ke(r), is Flemish for "little captain," as the Schipperke often rode on canal boats acting as guard. Either they are born without tails or the tails are removed at birth. The foxlike head is set off with a large ruff around the neck. The dog has a lively, curious, mischievous expression, and is fond of children, often acting as nurse. The body is short and thick-set, the coat very full and a solid glossy black. Weight up to 18 pounds.

Schipperke

OBEDIENCE
TRAINING
AND TESTS

Obedience Training and Tests The American Kennel Club has formulated rules and regulations regarding obedience tests which have become very popular with the public. The awards are C.D., meaning Companion Dog; C.D.X., Companion Dog Excellent; U.D., Utility Dog; and U.D.T., Utility Dog Tracking. Any dog winning these awards well deserves them as the competition is keen and the standards are high.

The Novice Class tests are: (1) to heel on leash; (2) to heel free; (3) to come when called; (4) to sit for one minute away from handler; (5) to lie down for three minutes away from handler. Points won in these classes count toward C.D. If the dog wins 85 points at each of three trials in which six or more dogs compete in the Novice Classes he wins the C.D. degree.

After receiving the C.D. the dog is eligible for the Open Class for the title of C.D.X. Here he must (1) heel on leash; (2) heel free; (3) drop on recall; (4) retrieve dumbbell on flat; (5) retrieve dumbbell over obstacle; (6) make a long jump; (7) sit for three minutes; (8) lie down for five minutes. When a dog has scored 220 or more points in each of three trials with six or more contestants, he is given his C.D.X. The dog must be taught to jump for distance and height and pick up and bring back to handler a specific object. The size and weight of the dumbbell for all large dogs is 16 ounces and for smaller breeds eight ounces. For the high jump the obstacle must be 3½ feet high for all large breeds; the smaller breeds must clear an obstacle twice their height at shoulder. The distance for broad jumping is four to six feet according to size of the dog.

For the Utility Dog title a contestant must speak on command, exercise scent discrimination, find lost articles, and stand for examination. For U.D.T. he must pass a "tracking" test in the open country. Both these awards are great honors.

The obedience tests help a dog overcome bad manners and really make him into a companion, one that the owner and all his friends can enjoy.

Obedience Jumping, German Shepherds

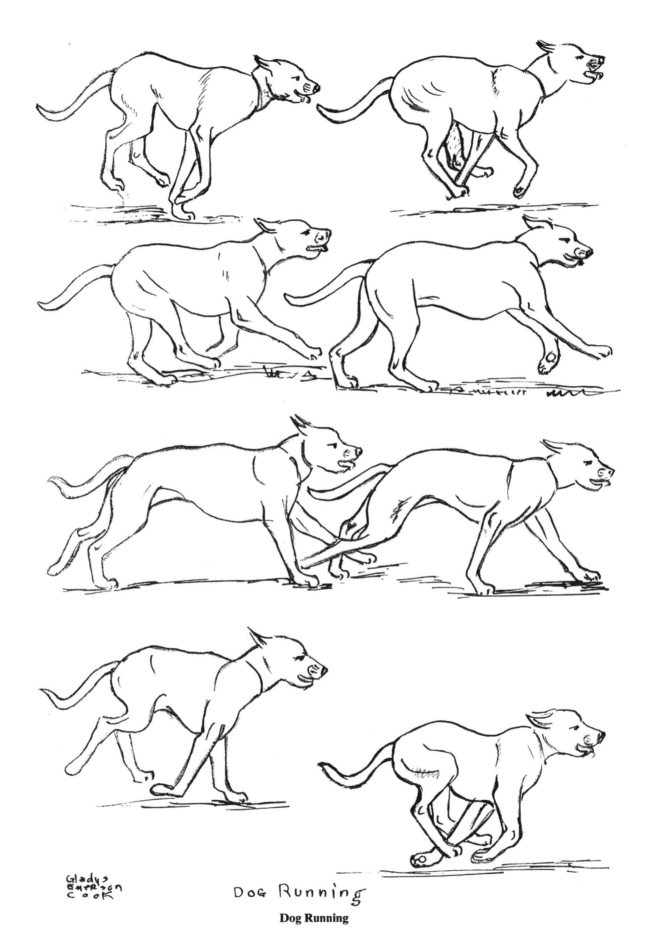

Dog Running

Dog Running

DOGS AND THEIR OWNERS

Where the picture representing a breed is not identified, the dog shown is an anonymous champion.

Sporting Dogs

Pointer, American, *Ch. Tyler's Showfield Sugar*. Floyd Evans, S. Grand Avenue, Pasadena, Calif.

German Shorthaired Pointer, *Ch. Robin Crest Chip*. Robin Crest Kennel, Alpine Drive, Armonk, N.Y.

German Wirehaired Pointer, *Ch. Oldmill's Casanova*. Mr. and Mrs. N. L. Compere, Lake Forest, Ill.

Chesapeake Bay Retriever, *Ch. Eastern Waters' Tallapoosa*, C.D. Mrs. Daniel Horn, Frenchtown, N.J.

Flat-Coated Retriever, *Ch. Bramcroft Dandy*, U.D. Mr. and Mrs. Gordon Terroux, Morrison, Colo.

Golden Retriever, *Ch. Prince Royal of Los Altos*. Oliver Wilhelm, Palo Alto, Calif.

Labrador Retriever, English and American Champion, *Sam of Blaircourt*. Mrs. G. B. Lambert, Princeton, N.J.

Yellow Labrador Retriever, *Ch. Whyger Gold Bullion*. Mrs. Frank Ginnel, Bedford Hills, N.Y.

English Setter, American and Canadian *Ch. Skidby's Sturdy Tyke*. Mr. and Mrs. E. J. Stacey, Glenburnie, Ontario, Canada.

Gordon Setter, *Ch. Gordon Hill Holly*, C.D. Mrs. Roland Clement, South Norwalk, Conn.

Irish Setter, *Ch. Michael Bryan Duke of Sussex*. Mrs. Oreen Peters, Detroit, Mich.

Irish Setter and pups, *Ch. My Wild Irish Rose*. Dr. Wolfgang Casper, Staten Island, N.Y.

Brittany Spaniel, *Ch. Duke du Danielle*. Daniel Miller, Williamsville, N.Y.

Clumber Spaniel, *Thornville Suzette*. Arlene Miller, Eatontown, N.J.

Black Cocker Spaniel, *Ch. Clarkdale Capitol Stock*. Elizabeth Clark, Deerfield, Ill.

Parti-Colored Cocker Spaniel, *Ch. Fraclin Colonel Caridas*. Mrs. Clinton Bishop, Fraclin Kennels, Collegeville, Pa.

ASCOB Black and Tan Cocker Spaniel, *Ch. Champagne's Caprice*. Dorothy Angerame, Westbury, N.Y.   (P. 19)

ASCOB Black and Tan Cocker Spaniel, Dog of the Year, 1961, *Ch. Pinetops Fancy Parade*. William Laffoon, Jr., and Mrs. Rose Robbins, Petersburg, Va. (P. 21)

English Cocker Spaniel, *Ch. Squirrel Run Burgomaster*. Mrs. Hallock Dupont, Wilmington, Del.

English Springer Spaniel, *Ch. Salilyn's MacDuff*. Mr. and Mrs. William Randall, Melothian, Ill.

Irish Water Spaniel, *Ch. Watergate's Lover Boy Casey*. Mr. and Mrs. J. M. Kennedy, Spencerport, N.Y.

Welsh Springer Spaniel, *Ch. Dien Glynie of Randhaven*. H. R. Randolph, Medford Station, N.Y.

Head of Welsh Springer Spaniel puppy. H. R. Randolph, Medford Station, N.Y.

Vizsla, *Ch. Duchess of Shirbob*, C.D. Comdr. Walter R. Campbell, USN, Long Beach, Calif.

Weimaraner, American and Canadian *Ch. Durmar's Karl*. Durwood Van Zandt, Rochester, N.Y.

Hounds

Afghan Hound, *Ch. Crown Crest Mr. Universe*. Kay Finch, Crown Crest Kennels, Corona Del Mar, Calif.

Afghan Hound, large head study, *Ch. Taejon of Crown Crest*, record holder. Kay Finch, Crown Crest Kennels, Corona Del Mar, Calif.

Basenji, *Ch. Bettina's Oribi*. Bettina Belmont Ward, Middleburg, Va.

Basset Hound, *Ch. The Ring's Banshee*. Chris Teeter, Birmingham, Mich.

Beagle, 15", *Ch. Page Mill Tumbleweed*. Dr. Aaron Leavitt, Longmeadow, Mass.

Beagle, 13", *Ch. Wandering Cinderella*. Mrs. Gordon, Los Gatos, Calif.

Bloodhound, *Ch. King Cole* full figure and head study. Mrs. Hartley Dodge, Madison, N.J.

Borzoi, *Ch. Sascha of Baronoff*. Mr. W. J. McCloskey, Wenonah, N.J.

Smooth Dachshund, *Ch. White Gables Ristocrat*. Mrs. Albert Van Court, Los Angeles, Calif.

Longhaired Dachshund, *Ch. Crespi's Happy New Year*. Charles and Donia Cline, Los Angeles, Calif.

Wirehaired Dachshund, *Ch. Happy Go Lucky of Willow Creek*. Elizabeth Holmberg, Holmdachs Kennels, Matawan, N.J.

Miniature Dachshund, *Ch. DeSangpur Wee Lancelot*. Mrs. William Burr Hill, Hicksville, N.Y.

Greyhound, *Ch. Rudel's Solitaire*. Dr. Elsie S. Neustadt, Quincy, Mass.

Irish Wolfhound, *Ch. Sir Gelert of Ambleside*. Barbara O'Neill, South Nyack, N.Y.

Norwegian Elkhound, *Ch. Tortasen's Bjonn II*. Mr. and Mrs. Wells Peck, Pitch Road Kennels, Litchfield, Conn.

Otterhound, *Ch. Lugina's Viking*. L. W. Fry, Gloversville, N.Y.

Rhodesian Ridgeback, *Ch. Rock-ridge's Temba* and *Ch. Rock-ridge's Fair Lady* (both from South Africa). Lamarde Perro Kennel, Freeland and Margaret Lowthian, Alpine, Calif.

Saluki, *Ch. Ahbou Farouk of Pine Paddocks.* Mrs. W. H. Freelan, Memphis, Tenn.

Working Dogs

Alaskan Malamute, *Ch. Dobuk May-Glen's Ochlach.* Mrs. John Fleet, Scotch Plains, N.J.

Belgian Tervuren, *Ch. Fidelité de Fauve Charbonne.* Dorothy Hollister, Middleville, Mich.

Bouvier des Flandres, *Ch. Argus de la Thudinie.* Deewal Kennels, Dorothy and Fred Walsh, Frenchtown, N.J.

Boxer, *Ch. Salgray's Battle Chief.* Daniel Hamilburg, Brookline, Mass.

Briard, *Ch. Fripon des Hersutes.* Mrs. William Morrison, Bristol, R.I.

Bullmastiff, *Ch. Pridzor's Anton of Buttonoak.* R. L. Twitty, Mount Vernon, N.Y.

Longhaired Collie, *Ch. Brand-wyne Needless to Say.* Dr. and Mrs. J. H. Mangels, Brand-wyne Kennels, New Milford, Conn.

Smooth-coated Collie, *Ch. Shamrock Smooth Rocket,* C.D.X. Gail Thompson, Yonkers, N.Y.

Doberman Pinscher, *Ch. Mar Bud's Tucky Miss.* Bud and Mary Cosgrove, Jeffersonville, Ind.

German Shepherd Dog, *Ch. Alf von Loherfeld.* Mrs. M. M. Dominick, Sharon, Conn.

Great Dane, *Ch. Honey Bun of Marydane.* Erna Huber, Brewster, N.Y.

Newfoundland, *Ch. Dryad's Conversation Piece.* Mrs. Kitty Drury, Phelps, N.Y.

Old English Sheepdog, *Ch. Fezziwig Ceiling Zero.* Hendrick Van Rensselaer, Basking Ridge, N.J.

Puli, *Ch. Skysyl Captivating Nancy.* Mary Bell Devlin, Pine Path Puli Kennels, Baltimore, Md.

Rottweiler, *Ch. Gerhardt von Stahl.* Mrs. Bernard Freeman, Manhasset, L.I. Breeders, Lurline and William Stahl.

Samoyed brace, *Int. Ch. Mishpa's Arctic Sue,* C.D., and *Int. Ch. Puoler Princess III of Loralee.* Mrs. Leo Poirier, Highland Park, Mich.

St. Bernard, *Ch. Harvey's Zwingo Barri V Banz.* Mrs. George Harvey, Syracuse, Ind.

Standard Schnauzer, *Ch. Patundlis Rigo.* Patundlis Kennels, Stillwater, N.J.

Shetland Sheepdog, *Ch. Pixie Dell Royal Blue.* A. R. Miller, Scarsdale, N.Y.

Siberian Husky, *Ch. Monadnock's Pando.* Mr. and Mrs. Nicholas Demidoff, Fitzwilliam, N.H.

Siberian Husky head study, *Ch. Markay's Aral's Bourbon.* Mary Buckley, Markay Kennels, Bethesda, Md.

Cardigan Welsh Corgi, *Ch. Lord Jim's Lucky Domino.* J. S. Churchill, Jr., New York, N.Y.

Pembroke Welsh Corgi, *Ch. Willets Red Jacket.* Mrs. W. B. Long, Carlisle, Mass.

Terriers

Airedale Terrier, *Ch. Bengal Sabu.* Barbara Strebeigh, Tuck Dell, and Harold Florsheim. Handler, Katherine Gately, Wilton, Conn.

Australian Terrier, *Ch. Cooees Straleon Aussie.* Mrs. Nell Fox, Mount Pleasant, N.J.

Bedlington Terrier, *Ch. Center Ridge Lady Caroline.* Robert Scherff, Center Ridge Kennels, Milwaukee, Wis.

Border Terrier, *Ch. Bruce.* Mrs. Marion Scott, Montpelier Station, Va.

Bull Terrier, *Ch. Radar of Monty-Ayr.* Dr. H. R. Doble, Baltimore, Md.

Cairn Terrier, *Ch. Moonstone of Killybracken.* Charlotte Fredericksen, Morrison, Colo.

Dandie Dinmont Terrier, *Ch. Gilespin B. Brown.* Anne Johnston, Brooklyn, N.Y.

Smooth Fox Terrier, *Ch. Battlecry Biff.* Mrs. Stewart Simmons, Bryn Mawr, Pa.

Wirehaired Fox Terrier, *Ch. Hetherington Treasure.* Mrs. T. H. Carruthers, III, Glendale, Ohio.

Kerry Blue Terrier, *Ch. Kerry-croft's Mr. O'Rourke.* Mrs. Nancy Christ, Boyertown, Pa.

Lakeland Terrier, *Ch. Tithebarn Limelight.* Mr. and Mrs. Robert Wiel, Kerryall Kennels, San Francisco, Calif.

Norwich Terrier, *Ch. Upland Spring Jock II.* Mrs. Howe Low, Philadelphia, Pa.

Miniature Schnauzer, *Ch. Yankee Pride Col. Stump.* Mrs. Joseph Sailer, Philadelphia, Pa.

Scottish Terrier, *Ch. Blanart Bewitching.* Blanche E. Reeg, Wantaugh, N.Y.

Sealyham Terrier, *Ch. Robin Hill Brigade.* Mrs. Robert B. Choate, Robin Hill Sealyhams, Danvers, Mass.

Skye Terrier, *Ch. Evening Star de Luchar.* Walter Goodman, New York, N.Y.

Staffordshire Terrier, *Ch. Rip Rock Irish Mike.* Rip Rock Kennels, Kay and Oscar Marusick, Clinton, Md.

Welsh Terrier, *Ch. Caradac Llwyd of St. Aubrey.* Mrs. Edward Alker, Great Neck, N.Y.

West Highland White Terrier, *Ch. Elfinbrook Simon,* Best in Show, Westminster, 1962. Barbara Worcester, Little Falls, N.J.

Toys

Affenpinscher, *Ch. Aff-Airn Rody.* Mrs. Arthur Harrington, Aff-Airn Kennels, Rensselaer, N.Y.

Smooth Chihuahua, *Ch. Luce's Flash-E-Gaylo.* Mrs. Rozel Luce, Kennedy, N.Y.

Longhaired Chihuahua, *Ch. Lane's Prince Rojalio.* Ruth Lane, Mokena, Ill.

Brussels Griffon, American and Canadian Champion, *Buka Proctor.* R. William Taylor and Nigel-Aubrey Jones, Montreal, Que., Canada.

118

Italian Greyhound, *Ch. Winterlea Piero*. Mrs. Freeman Gosden, Beverly Hills, Calif.

Japanese Spaniel, *Ch. Nippon Airashii San*. Mrs. D. H. Rogers, Kingston, Ont., Canada.

Maltese, *Ch. Talia of Villa Malta*. Dr. and Mrs. Vincenzo Calvaresi, Villa Malta Kennels, Bedford, Mass.

Toy Manchester Terrier, *Ch. Grenadier Ragtime Rhythm Boy*. Rodney Herner, Pottstown, Pa.

Papillon, *Ch. Little Queen of Pinqueny*. Sallie Pinckney, Hightstown, N.J.

Pekingese, *Int. Ch. Calartha Mandarin of Jehol*. Mrs. Vera F. Crofton, Topanga, Calif.

Miniature Pinscher, *Ch. Rebel Roc's Casanova Von Kurt*. Mrs. E. W. Tipton, Jr., Kingsport, Tenn.

Pomeranian, *Ch. Rider's Sparklin' Gold Nugget*. Mr. and Mrs. Porter Washington, Beverly Hills, Calif.

Toy Poodle, *Ch. Nibroc's Gary*. Smilestone Kennels, Morristown, N.J.

Pug, *Tri. Int. Ch. Pugville's Mighty Jim*. Mrs. Filomena Doherty, Pugville Kennels, Bernardsville, N.J.

Pug, black, *Ch. Ken-Lu Prides Diplomat*. Mrs. Florence Bartels, Astoria, N.Y.

Pug puppies. Mrs. Filomena Doherty, Pugville Kennels, Bernardstown, N.J.

Yorkshire Terrier, English and American Champion *Buranthea's Doutelle*. Mrs. Leslie Gordon, Jr., and Miss J. Bennett, Glenview, Ill.

Non-Sporting Dogs

Boston Terrier, *Ch. B-B's Kim of Fellow*. Mrs. Celeste Schulte, Cincinnati, Ohio.

Bulldog, *Ch. Vardona's Frosty Snowman*. Dr. Edward Vardon, Vardona Kennels, Detroit, Mich.

Chow Chow, *Ch. Ah Sid's The Dilettante*. Ah Sid Kennels, Gaithersburg, Md.

Dalmatian, *Ch. Racing Roadster in the Valley*. Mr. and Mrs. S. K. Allman, Jr., Doylestown, Pa.

Dalmatian puppies. Some from kennels of Wayne L. Smith, Greenwich, Conn.

French Bulldog, *Ch. Ralanda Ami Francine*. Mr. and Mrs. Ralph West, Livonia, Mich.

Keeshond, *Ch. Wil Los Jamie Boy*. William and Lois McNamara, Silver Spring, Md.

Lhasa Apso, *Ch. Licos Kulu La*. Mrs. John Licos, Beverly Hills, Calif.

Standard Poodle, *Ch. Donna of Westford-Ho*. Mrs. Anna Mosher, Harmo Kennels, Amherst, N.H.

Miniature Poodle, *Ch. Estid Ballet Dancer*. Col. Ferguson, Hollywood, Calif.

Schipperke, *Ch. Lo-Lane Denise*. Doris Giles, Philadelphia, Pa.

INDEX